EXPLORE
BERLIN

by Patricia Hutchison

12 STORY LIBRARY
MORE TO EXPLORE

www.12StoryLibrary.com

12-Story Library is an imprint of Bookstaves.

Photographs ©: Subodh Agnihotri/Shutterstock.com, cover, 1; N.M.Bear/Shutterstock.com, 4; Stavros Argyropoulos/Shutterstock.com, 5; PD, 6; Nick Fox/Shutterstock.com, 6; Alberto Loyo/Shutterstock.com, 7; hanohiki/Shutterstock.com, 8; Boris-B/Shutterstock.com, 9; SpandowStockPhoto/Shutterstock.com, 10; astudio/Shutterstock.com, 11; nito/Shutterstock.com, 12; Claudio Divizia/Shutterstock.com, 13; ESB Professional/Shutterstock.com, 14; Paceman/Shutterstock.com, 14; DisobeyArt/Shutterstock.com, 15; Jaroslav Moravcik/Shutterstock.com, 16; Ansgar Koreng/CC3.0, 17; Vlad1988/Shutterstock.com, 18; Juergen Nowak/Shutterstock.com, 19; Nattee Chalermtiragool/Shutterstock.com, 20; canadastock/Shutterstock.com, 21; AnikonaAnn/Shutterstock.com, 22; Superbass/CC4.0, 22; SergeyPhoto7/Shutterstock.com, 23; Cineberg/Shutterstock.com, 24; hanohiki/Shutterstock.com, 25; hanohiki/Shutterstock.com, 26; Roman Babakin/Shutterstock.com, 27; seeyah panwan/Shutterstock.com, 29

ISBN
9781632357229 (hardcover)
9781632358318 (paperback)
9781645820093 (ebook)

Library of Congress Control Number: 2019938644

Printed in the United States of America
September 2019

About the Cover

The Berlin skyline along the Spree River.

Access free, up-to-date content on this topic plus a full digital version of this book. Scan the QR code on page 31 or use your school's login at 12StoryLibrary.com.

Table of Contents

1

Berlin Is a City of Waterways

The Bode Museum along the Spree River.

Berlin lies in northeast Germany. It is the nation's capital and largest city. Berlin is a city–state surrounded by the state of Brandenburg. It is divided into 12 boroughs.

Berlin covers an area of 344 square miles (891 sq km). The land is mostly flat. The Spree River runs through it. In the western part of the city, the Spree empties into the Havel River. Berlin lies only 111 feet (34 m) above sea level. It has plenty of groundwater. Because of this, forests grow easily there.

The capital has many canals. Its low elevation makes it easy to dig them. The canals are used to transport goods around Berlin and other parts of Germany.

Berlin has a moderate climate. Winters are cold with little sunshine. Snow or freezing rain falls often. Temperatures can go below minus 4 degrees Fahrenheit (-20°C). Spring weather changes often. Some

Berliners often gather along the canals in the city.

days are warm. Others can feel like winter. In the summer, daytime temperatures are warm. The sky is usually sunny. But thunderstorms can pop up in the afternoon. The nights are cool.

1,700
Number of bridges in Berlin

- Besides two large rivers, the city also has many canals.
- The Berlin area has the largest network of waterways in Europe.
- The capital has more bridges than Venice.

BERLIN IS A UHI

Berlin is an urban heat island. A UHI is a metropolitan area that is warmer than the rural area around it. Berlin is often one to two degrees warmer than surrounding areas. During the day, people, cars, buses, and trains create heat energy. Nighttime temperatures stay high. Buildings trap the heat coming from the ground. It can't escape into the cool night sky.

2

A Capital Born, Divided, and Reunited

Berlin was founded in 1237. It arose from two trading towns. The city grew steadily. In 1701, Friedrich I of Prussia made Berlin his royal residence. Eight years later, he declared it the capital of the Prussian Kingdom.

Starting in the 1870s, the city had an economic boom. But the prosperity didn't last. During World War I (1914–1918), Allied forces blockaded German ports. Millions living in Berlin were starving. A revolution broke out against the government. In 1919, the constitutional monarchy was replaced by a democratic republic. Ten years later, the Great Depression hit the capital hard. There were violent demonstrations. Many people were killed or injured.

Adolf Hitler rose to power in 1933. Democracy ended in Germany. The first concentration camp was built in Berlin. It was a prison for people who challenged Hitler. World War II began in 1939. A year later, the first bomb was dropped on Berlin. When the war ended in 1945, the city was mostly rubble.

The capital was split into occupied zones. The eastern part was taken by the communist Soviet Union. The United States,

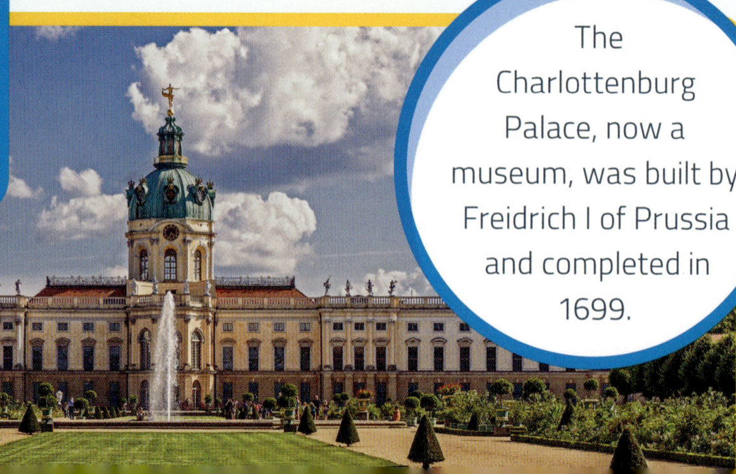

The Charlottenburg Palace, now a museum, was built by Freidrich I of Prussia and completed in 1699.

At least 171

Number of people killed trying to get over the Berlin Wall

- More than 5,000 people managed to cross the border between 1961 and 1989.
- Some climbed over the barbed wire.
- Others flew in hot air balloons or swam through the sewers underneath.

Britain, and France took charge of the western half. Many Germans were against communism. Thousands of East Germans crossed into West Berlin. In 1961, the communist government of East Germany built a wall dividing the city. Almost no one could cross to either side.

Twenty-eight years later, the policy changed. On November 9, 1989, citizens were allowed to cross the border. People used hammers and picks to destroy the wall. Berlin was finally reunited in 1990. Today it is a thriving city.

TIMELINE

1237: Berlin arises from two settlements on the Spree River.

1671: Berlin's Jewish community is founded.

1871: Berlin becomes the capital of the German Empire.

1933: Over 1,200 Jews are arrested during Kristallnacht, the Night of Broken Glass.

1943: Allied forces begin large-scale bombing of Berlin.

1945: Berlin is divided into two parts.

1961: A wall is built dividing East and West Berlin.

1989: The Berlin Wall is torn down, reuniting the two parts of Berlin.

2005: The Holocaust Memorial is unveiled.

A remnant of the Berlin Wall today.

3 Berliners Today

Berlin has a population of about 3.7 million people. It is the second most populous city in the European Union. The people call themselves Berliners. The capital is a multicultural city. Over 600,000 immigrants have come from 190 different countries.

German is the official language in Berlin. But other languages are spoken there as well. English, Turkish, Arabic, Russian, and Greek are heard. Asian languages are spoken. Some Berliners are upset that so many people in the city speak English. They think more people should speak German. Starting in 2016, refugees who want to stay in Germany must learn German. If they don't, they won't be able to stay in the country legally.

Berlin has a very diverse population.

Although Berlin is a bustling city, many people don't have jobs. The unemployment rate there is the

Art is a big part of the culture in Berlin.

highest in the nation. The city has a growing homeless population. They depend on many shelters across the city. In 2015, Berlin received more subsidies than any other part of Germany.

54

Percentage of people in Berlin under age 45

- Berlin is a young city.
- The average age of Berliners is around 42. Yet there are fewer people under 15 than over 65.
- Germany has the lowest birthrate in Europe.

After the fall of the Berlin Wall, housing was very affordable. Low rents brought artists and other creative types. Berlin still draws many artists and musicians today. The city attracts scientists, too. The capital is one of the largest regions for science in Europe. Many research facilities are located there.

THINK ABOUT IT

If you moved to a different country, would you want to learn the language? What are the advantages of doing that?

4 One of the World's Largest Economies

Seimens employs many people in its medical division.

Berlin is Germany's political center. Many Berliners work for the government. Berlin is also Germany's chief economic center. It is Europe's most powerful economy and the fourth-largest economy in the world. Manufacturing is an important industry. Large companies such as Siemens and Bayer produce medicines. Other businesses make machinery and electrical devices. These are Berlin's leading exports. The city also has a strong printing and paper industry.

GOVERNMENT FUNDING FOR RESEARCH

The government funds much of the research performed in Berlin. Some companies study ways to detect and prevent diseases. Others research new technologies. Many businesses work for the federal government. State governments fund more than 100 other organizations.

The service economy has become more important in recent years. Berlin is one of the most popular places to visit in Europe. More than 80 percent of all employees work in the service sector. Many work in restaurants and hotels. Tourism also creates jobs in transportation and entertainment.

Berlin is a center for science and research. Much of the research is done in the city's many universities. Scholars study environmental and life sciences. Medical research is important to Berlin's economy.

The city encourages new fields of technology. These include information and communication technologies. Berlin is leading the way in green technologies. Businesses there produce clean energy and develop ways to store it. They promote energy efficiency and water management.

300

Number of medical technology companies in Berlin

- The capital is an important location for the health care industry.
- Over 30 pharmaceutical companies are based there.
- The city has more than 130 hospitals.

Business in Berlin has a glamorous side as well. Filmmakers love Berlin. The capital has become one of Germany's most popular shooting locations. Superstars such as George Clooney and Cate Blanchett can often be seen filming in Berlin.

The service industry employs the most people.

5

Battered Buildings Are Given New Life

Berlin is a mixture of classical and modern architecture. Bombs destroyed many buildings during World War II. Some survived. Others have been restored. Centuries-old palaces stand among buildings designed by modern architects.

The Neue Wache was built in 1818. For a century, it served as a guardhouse for royal troops. Roman columns stand at the front. Sculptures near the roof show an ancient battle. The goddess of victory stands at the peak. Today the building is a place of remembrance. People go there to think about the victims of war and dictatorship.

Some old buildings have been given modern updates. The German Historical Museum dates from the 1600s, when it was used as an armory. The front has arched windows. Statues line the roof. In 2003, a modern extension was added. A glass and metal tower spirals up the back.

The Neue Wache.

The Philharmonie concert hall.

Architects turned to more contemporary styles after the fall of the Berlin Wall. The new Jewish Museum is a zigzag of glass and dark metal. The golden Philharmonie is home to the world-famous Berlin Philharmonic Orchestra. It has a curved, freeform design. The city's stock exchange building is known as the Armadillo. It is a modern steel and glass structure. Inspired by sports, the Square 3 includes three towers of gold, silver, and bronze. These are the colors of the Olympic medals. This development has updated the center of the city.

72

Number of acres in the Horseshoe Estate

- This development was built in the 1920s as public housing for low-income Berliners.
- The estate is an important example of modernist values and architecture.
- It is part of a UNESCO World Heritage Site.

THINK ABOUT IT

Sometimes it's easier to tear down an old building than update it. Why do you think Berlin wants to keep some of its old buildings around?

6

A Modern and Efficient Infrastructure

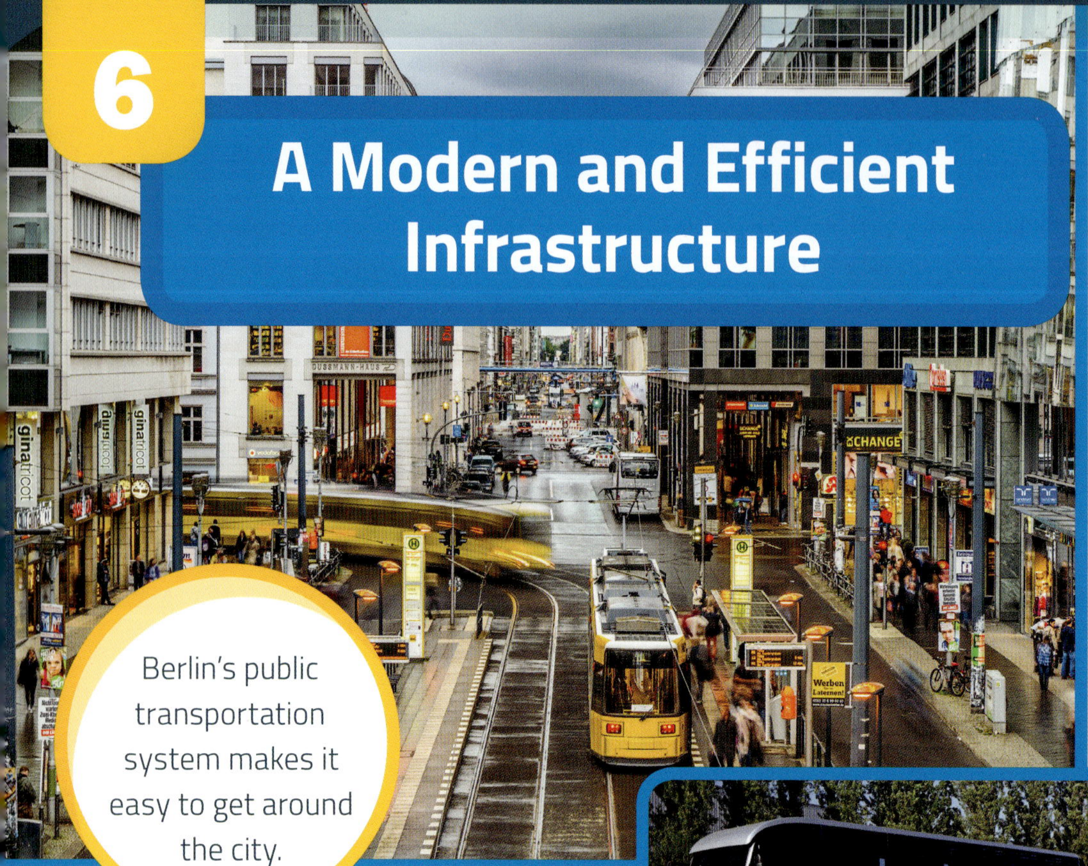

Berlin's public transportation system makes it easy to get around the city.

Berlin is a link between Eastern and Western Europe. The city is crossed by major trade and transportation routes. Its infrastructure is important to the entire region.

The Berlin Transport Company provides public transportation within the city. The Berlin Central Station is the main hub for rail traffic. There, city and regional trains connect with Berlin's huge and efficient public transport network.

An average of 3 million trips are taken by passengers each day. Several forms of transportation are available. These include the subway, light rail, buses, ferries, and trams. But even though many people use public transportation, the city still has the worst traffic jams in Germany.

Berlin has Germany's most modern communications system. It includes fiber optics and high-speed broadband. The city has had this infrastructure advantage for years.

One thing Berlin doesn't have is housing. There are not enough homes for its growing population. Affordable housing is especially hard to find. The government has promised to build almost 200,000 new homes by 2030. At least half will have affordable rents.

8.7

How many times each day Berlin's public transport system would circle the earth, if all the trips were laid end-to-end

- Together, all the parts of Berlin's transit system travel hundreds of thousands of miles daily.
- Many lines operate 24 hours a day.
- Ticket prices start at under $2.

TOWARD A GREENER INFRASTRUCTURE

Berlin is committed to becoming more bike-friendly. The city is developing 62 miles (100 km) of bicycle highways. Sturdy posts will be built along existing bike lanes. These will help prevent crashes and keep bikers safe. The capital will also create 100,000 new bike parking spots.

7

A Major Cultural Center

Berlin is home to many famous museums, opera houses, and theaters. Museum Island features five museums. The island is located in the Spree River. The Pergamon Museum on the island is the most visited in Berlin. It has art and treasures from the ancient Middle East. Other buildings showcase antiques, paintings, and sculptures. Together the museums' collections include 6,000 years of art.

Berlin was once the world's largest Jewish city. Visitors to the Jewish Museum can explore 2,000 years of Jewish history including letters from local Holocaust victims. Paintings and photographs are also on display.

Berlin is packed with art galleries. One of the most unusual is the Sammlung Boros. This is a private museum in a converted World War II bunker. The building still has bullet holes. All the art belongs to the owners. The only way to see it is by making an appointment far in advance. Guided tours for small groups take place on the weekends.

Opera fans enjoy visiting the Berlin State Opera. Berliners love opera so much the city hosts an opera

Victims of the Holocaust are remembered at the Jewish Museum.

The House of World Cultures is located in Tiergarten Park.

CHECKPOINT CHARLIE

Checkpoint Charlie was one of the locations where people could legally cross the wall into East Berlin. Today the Mauer Museum is there. Actors playing border guards stand outside. Inside are stories of people who tried to escape. Some were successful. Others were not.

festival each year called Festtage. Another music festival called Classic Open Air takes place outdoors in Gendarmenmarkt, a beautiful city square. The House of World Cultures features contemporary arts from around the world. People go there to see theater, dance, and art exhibitions. The building was a gift from the United States.

150

Approximate number of theaters in Berlin

- In the 1920s, Berlin was known as the City of Music and Theatre.
- There are nearly 170 museums in the city.
- Berlin has hundreds of art galleries.

8 Berlin Has Sports All Year Long

Berlin is often called Germany's capital of sports. The city has six professional teams and hosts many amateur matches. Spectators and participants can always find something to do. Football (soccer) is the national sport. Hertha BSC is the favorite pro team. Many businesses sponsor their own teams. There are leagues for amateurs.

The Eisbären Berlin ice hockey team has won several German titles. Eisbären is German for polar bear. ALBA Berlin is one of the most successful basketball teams in Europe. The city also has professional handball and volleyball teams.

Berliners love all types of racing. Germany's capital hosts the all-electric Formula E Championship. The race takes place each spring at the former airport. The cars race around a 1.47-mile (2.38 km) track. The Velothon Berlin is one of the largest bicycle races in Europe. The course offers two routes. Beginners travel 37 miles (60 km). Expert cyclists travel 62 miles (100 km). Both routes pass famous sites in Berlin.

The Hertha BSC team.

ISTAF (the International Stadium Festival) is the world's largest one-day athletic event. Nearly 200 athletes participate every year. These include world champions and Olympic medalists. The games feature different track and field events. They are held in the Berlin Olympic Stadium. Nearly 50,000 spectators attend.

TIME OUTDOORS

People in Berlin enjoy a variety of outdoor sports. During the warmer months, the city's parks buzz with activity. Families throw frisbees and play table tennis. Rock climbing walls are also popular. Clubs around the city offer polo and golf.

40,000

Number of athletes who take part in the Berlin Marathon

- They come from over 100 different counties.
- Bands and dance groups cheer the runners on.
- There are separate races for wheelchair racers, cyclists, and inline skaters.

9

A City of Attractions Old and New

Brandenburg Gate is one of Berlin's most important monuments. The grand columns were built in 1791. The gate was a symbol of the divided city. In 1987, US President Ronald Reagan gave a famous speech there. He urged Mikhail Gorbachev, the leader of the Soviet Union, to tear down the Berlin Wall. After it fell in 1989, Brandenburg Gate became Berlin's symbol of unity.

Another famous site is the Charlottenburg Palace. It was built during the 1600s for Queen Charlotte of Prussia. Visitors are amazed by the collections of china and paintings on display. The palace stands in a beautiful garden beside the river Spree.

Several attractions are reminders of WWII. The Soviet War Memorial honors Soviet

Brandenburg Gate symbolizes unity for the city.

The Berlin TV Tower.

216.5

Height in feet (66 m) of Viktoriapark Falls

- Viktoriapark is a large green space in the middle of Berlin.
- The falls are the city's tallest natural elevation.
- In the winter, locals love to sled down the hill inside the park.

soldiers who died. The huge statue shows a soldier stepping on a crushed swastika. The East Side Gallery is a mile-long (1.6 km) section of the Berlin Wall that is still standing. Artists came from all over the world to paint on it. Over 100 paintings capture the world's joy over the end of the Cold War era.

The Berlin Television Tower shows the capital's modern side. Standing 1,207 feet (368 m), it is Berlin's tallest building. It can be seen from anywhere in the city. A revolving restaurant at the top gives a 360-degree view. The Berlin Zoo is another popular attraction. It has more species of animals than any other zoo in the world. Visitors can see African penguins, American bison, and Australian red kangaroos. In 2017, the zoo welcomed Jiao Qing and Meng Meng, giant pandas from China. They are the only pandas in Germany.

10 Berliners Love Sausage

Schnitzel (left) and Currywurst are Berlin's favorite dishes.

Germans love meat, potatoes, and sauces. Their food is hearty and comforting. Schnitzel is a famous national dish. A thin piece of veal is covered with bread crumbs and fried. Modern takes on schnitzel use chicken or tofu. Either way, it is always served with potatoes.

Currywurst is a favorite dish in Berlin. Sausage is grilled and cut into slices. Then it's smothered in a sauce made with ketchup, Worcestershire sauce, and curry powder. The dish is so important it once had its own museum. Samples were served at the end of the tour.

Eisben is a classic Berlin dish. Pork knuckles are boiled or grilled. They are served with sauerkraut, peas, and potatoes. Spaetzle is Germany's style of pasta. The dough is made from eggs, flour, salt, and fizzy water. It is shaped into little dumplings, boiled, and served with loads of cheese. Berliners' favorite dessert is ice cream. Long lines form at outdoor stands even on cold winter days.

Berlin is a shoppers' delight. It has something for everyone. Department stores, malls, and small shops line the streets of the capital. Frederick Street is Berlin's main shopping area. Stores sell clothing, cosmetics, and jewelry.

KaDeWe is a famous upscale store in Berlin. The name is short for Kaufhaus des Westens. The huge store has beautiful displays. It sells hundreds of luxury products. Humana is the opposite of KaDeWe. It also has a huge selection of clothing and jewelry. But everything is secondhand and reasonably priced.

1891

Year when the Markthalle IX street food market opened

- The market is held once a week in the large Kreuzberg hall.
- Crowds of locals and visitors flock to the market.
- Vendors sell everything from Chinese noodles to international cheeses.

The KaDeWe store is a shopper's paradise.

11

Daily Life Is Casual

Germans are known for being on time. But Berliners tend to be more relaxed. To them, it's okay to be a few minutes late. Business clothing is more casual. Men and women rarely wear suits, unless they work for more traditional companies.

Many commuters in Berlin like to bicycle to work. This is especially true when the weather is sunny. But some also ride in cold, rainy weather. When the streets become too snowy, they return to public transport.

Berlin commuters bicycle to work year-round.

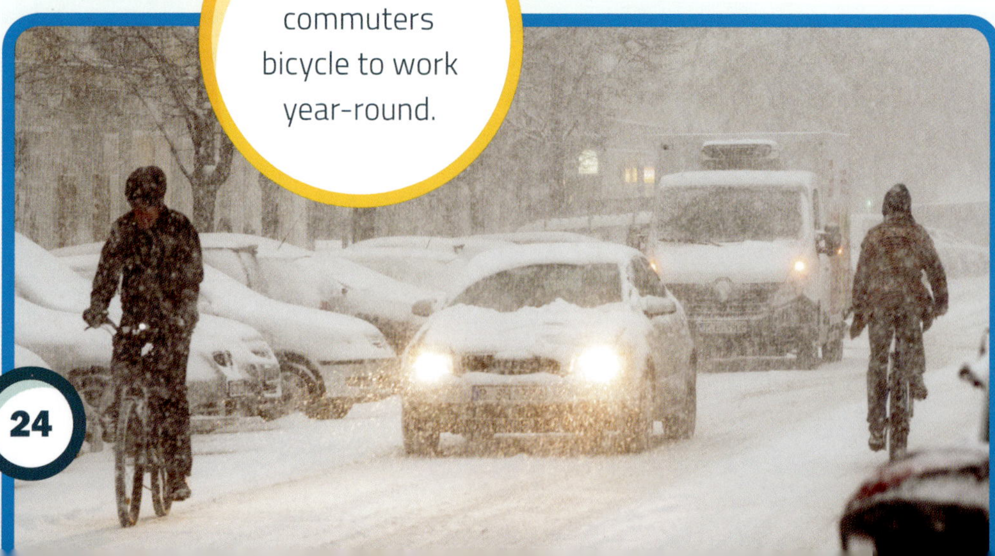

Most students in Berlin attend public schools. Public education is free, including university. Children aged three to six go to kindergarten. School is required until age 16. Classes start around 7:30 a.m. They end between noon and 1 p.m. Elementary students study reading, writing, and math. After fourth grade, they are separated into different types of secondary schools.

Berliners are big on recycling. Their system helps the environment and the people. Grocery stores have

435

Average number of people who move into Berlin each day

- Meanwhile, an average of 327 people move out of the city each day.
- More people in and fewer people out makes it difficult to find a place to live.
- Berliners move often. Each hour, an average of 20 people relocate to a different neighborhood.

recycling machines. People put their empty bottles in. A small amount of money comes out.

THINK ABOUT IT

Berliners like to recycle. How would you rate your city or town on its recycling efforts? What can you do to help?

People in the capital love their downtime. When temperatures are warm, they flock to the parks. They like to picnic and relax in the fresh air. On weekend nights, the clubs are filled. Adults dance to techno music until the early hours of the morning.

Berliners love to spend time in their parks.

12

Fairs, Festivals, and Fun

There is always something to celebrate in Berlin. International Green Week is one of the biggest agricultural fairs in the world. The festivities take place in mid-January. Fairgoers enjoy food tastings and forestry exhibits. They also learn a lot. Displays show where their food comes from. People attend classes on the latest food trends.

The Spring Festival takes place at the end of March. Visitors enjoy food, live music, and fireworks. There are shows and amusement

The Carnival of Cultures Parade is open to everybody and all forms of cultural expression.

1990

Year when the Unification Treaty was signed

- The treaty declared an end to the division of Germany into East and West.
- It named October 3 as the Day of German Unity, a national holiday.
- Berliners celebrate with a street festival that offers food, drinks, and fun.

Christmas markets in December are filled with all kinds of holiday treats.

rides for kids. May brings International Museum Day. Many Berlin museums give special tours. The event helps raise awareness of how museums add to the city's culture.

May also brings the Carnival of Cultures. Several music stages feature acts from around the world. Vendors sell food and handmade crafts. There is a huge street parade. People from over 80 different countries participate.

Oktoberfest has been celebrated in Berlin since 1949. Brass bands play under a huge party tent. People eat pork knuckles and pretzels. Families ride bumper cars and merry-go-rounds. They dance and play darts.

CHRISTMAS MARKETS

In December, streets in Berlin are lined with Christmas markets. The most popular one sits in front of the Charlottenburg Palace. Vendors sell handmade nativity scenes and tree ornaments. The scents of gingerbread and baking bread put people in the holiday spirit.

Fun Facts about Berlin

- Area: 344 square miles (891 sq km).
Population in 2018: 3.7 million.
- Vending machines in Berlin sell everything from gold bars to ballet shoes.
- Each year, Berlin hosts one of the largest New Year's Eve celebrations in the world. Nearly one million people attend.
- Outside of Turkey, Berlin has the world's largest Turkish population.
- The Berlin Zoo hosts 1,400 different animal species and over 20,000 animals. It has the largest number of species in the world.
- Berlin is home to three active, world-class opera houses. Together they can accommodate over 4,400 audience members.
- More than 44 percent of the city is green spaces. These include waterways, woods, rivers, and parks.
- Berlin has more museums than rainy days.

Where in the World?

Glossary

armory
A place where weapons are kept.

blockade
An act of sealing off a place to prevent people or goods from entering or leaving.

city–state
A city and surrounding state that has its own government.

Cold War era
A time of tension between the Soviet Union and the United States.

communism
A political system in which all property is owned by the people, and people are paid according to their abilities.

constitutional monarchy
A form of government where the king or queen shares power with a government organized by a constitution.

fiber optics
A method of transmitting information by sending pulses of light through thin, flexible fibers of glass.

infrastructure
The basic organizational and physical structures needed to operate a city, such as roads, buildings, power supplies, and communication systems.

metropolitan
A city and the densely populated areas around it.

pharmaceutical
Relating to medical drugs.

republic
A form of government where the power is held by the people and their elected representatives.

sector
An area that is separate from others.

subsidy
Money given by a government to help support something good for the public.

traditional
Something that has been established for a long time.

Read More

Doeden, Matt. *The Berlin Wall: An Interactive Modern History Adventure.* Mankato, MN: Capstone Press, 2015.

Nielsen, Jennifer A. *A Night Divided.* New York: Scholastic, 2015.

Tunnell, Michael O. *Candy Bomber: The Story of the Berlin Airlift's "Chocolate Pilot."* Watertown, MA: Charlesbridge, 2010.

Index

About the Author

Patricia Hutchison is a former teacher. She has written dozens of nonfiction children's books about science, nature, history, and geography. She lives in South Carolina with her husband. They love to travel throughout the United States and to other countries.